Kate Liberty

Golden

Retriever

Care

A Complete Guide to Learn How to Take Care of Your Golden Retriever. Diet, Health, Behavior, Training

Table of Contents

Golden Retriever Information You Should Know

If you are considering a pet that would be able to offer loyalty, obedience, and great entertainment, Golden Retriever would be the right choice for you. It is one of the most popular breeds in the world. Golden Retrievers have their origin in Britain. Initially, they were considered hunters as well as water perdiguero dogs; their coats are waterproof. Female pilgrims weigh about 55-65 pounds and males 65-75 pounds. The size of females and males is about 21 to 23 inches and 23 to 24 inches, respectively. The breed is large, powerful, and energetic. Do not let their cute and innocent face fool you; they are known as very intelligent and obedient dogs. The beautiful cream or golden color of his coat is the source of his name.

Information about the breed became abundant and was officially recognized in 1920 as a Golden Retriever. In 1927, Canada became the first country to register and authorize the breeding of the Golden retriever breed. In 1958, his club was named The Golden Retriever Club of Canada.

One of the most common types of goldens is the British, also known as the English Partridge dog. It is usually found in European and Australian countries. Its muzzle is wider and shorter, and the forehead slightly more block. They have shorter legs, a deeper chest, and a shorter tail. Male grouse dogs of this type have a height of between 56 centimeters and 61 centimeters and while their female counterparts have a height of between 51 and 56 centimeters. American varieties of goldens are lankier and less hardy than the English breed. Canadiandogs are very similar to the American breed. In color, they are usually a darker shade. English varieties have many unique and lighter shades of cream and gold, as well as rare white. A common and distinctive feature of All Golden Retrievers is the fact that their tails do not bend.

In adulthood, a minimum of care for goldens is required. Preparation is the most important aspect of adult retriever care. Weekly maintenance should include brushing your coat twice a week, cutting messy hair, and cleaning your ears. Although dogs are very abundant, they are susceptible to ear infections.

Golden Retrievers are considered as poor as guardian dogs. This is because of his friendly approach to strangers. They are stable, kind, and loving. They like to receive and pay attention. Dogs of this breed are faithful and devoted. They are well-bred, sensitive nature, as well as playful type. Their kindness to humans, especially children, and other dogs is excellent. They are easily trained animals and obey their manipulators. They are immensely friendly with children, adults, and other dogs.

Goldens can perform such exercises as dog agility. They are good facilitators because of their learning abilities and hardworking nature. Intelligence made them very famous. They have a higher level of patience and do not instantly irritate. They are very concerned about their task. They obey their caregivers. This breed was the first winner of the AKC Obedience test champion. They are very competitive at different events. This breed will easily respond to different training styles. They are famous as mobility assistance dogs, guide dogs and search dogs, as well as rescue dogs

This breed is affected by a common disease called hip dysplasia. Care should be taken in diet and exercise to keep an animal healthy. Cancer is the most common disease that can lead to death. Other diseases common to this breed are eye inflammations, heart and joint diseases, skin and Lyme diseases and hemophilia.

Golden Retrievers are extremely compassionate and intelligent animals that make excellent animals for any family, regardless of their age. Keep yourself well-groomed with Gold, love, and caress as much as possible, and you will have a welcome family member for many years.

What Makes Golden Retrievers So Popular?

The first initial impression, when you see an adult Golden Retriever or puppy for the case, is the attractive, very affectionate, and friendly, as well as noisy, especially when he is young. They are exceptionally loyal and eager to please their owner, very playful, and are quite obedient when properly trained.

This breed of dog is extremely popular among young or single families, which has a lot to do with their loyalty and affectionate nature. While everyone wants them as a pet should also be willing to commit to their needs, including proper exercise, especially if they have a small yard, house, or apartment. With proper nutrition, care, and regular exercise, they are more likely to live a long and healthy life.

The Golden Retriever usually gives the appearance of confidence as seen visibly in its physical characteristics. They have a strong athletic body and bold posture. It is in addition to their personality and temperament to make them affectionate and calm; their interaction with other people is obvious. They also tend to get along with other dogs and pets they encounter. Its general characteristics are the soft, feathered outer layer that can be straight or wavy. The undercoat is waterproof, although they tend to throw fur all year round and even more so during the warmer months. Regular grooming prevents overflows during the summer while keeping coats free of tangles or tangles.

Due to their temperament, training abilities, and intelligence, the Golden Retrievers were also popular as work or service dogs, as a guide dog for the blind, as well as search and rescue. They were also great companions or visitors of the elderly in retirement homes.

They are sociable and very extroverted animals. Their passionate disposition makes them the ideal dog breed; they are quite patient and very kind to young children. Which only emphasizes that they are safe family pets to have. They can be very excitable and need to be supervised in the presence of young children and newborns, as they can shoot them down by chance.

Golden Retrievers are usually not aggressive, but it is worth checking their history and good breeding and breeding as puppies, as they may have developed unwanted aggression. They are generally known as village animals because they like to spend time around people instead of being left alone. Sometimes going out for long periods of time can also attract your aggression instead of being with a lot of people.

Although they are not widely considered a watchdog, they have a bellows bark. They are always welcome to new visitors and satisfy those around them.

Golden retrievers have been a very popular pet for years, their loving nature and training ability makes it an ideal family pet for you and popular as one of the best family dog breeds.

Golden Retriever Breeder

The Golden Retrievers, the youngest of the retriever breeds and the most capricious of all. With their wavy, not really golden fur, of course, soft and powerful facial expressions combined with their unique and infamous ability to hunt and recover, you can understand why they are so popular. Therefore, if you are going to have one, you first need to know what to look for in a good Golden Retriever breeder.

Today, there are many people looking for smart dogs, can train easily, while they have a good appearance, that this type of dog literally owns. The first thing you should know about a good breeder is that you should have a good understanding of the history of how the breed was born.

I don't want to know everything about his background literally, because he'll look like a dog breed historian. Perhaps a clue how the breed has its good looks and talents apart from other dogs. Another is that he or she should know the standard appearance, size, and weight of Pilgrim dogs. Its structure, shape, walking, standing, and sitting should be taken into account. He is a gold coat, along with his talents and abilities. However, it is the thing at the highest price.

Toilet, yes, this is an important part that should be taken into account when buying such a dog. The Golden Retrievers lose their coat a lot. This is the first question people ask when buying a new dog. You could even fill an entire pillowcase with just your hair! Another is about health problems, as the perverted dog usually encounters several health problems and which remedies are best.

The dog's temperament and training ability are important. If a person is going to buy a Golden Retriever, they are usually looking for puppies, a month, or more. A breeder cannot yet be sure of his temperament, but he should be able to tell the buyer the usual temperament of puppy shows.

But this is still what people think of the Golden Retrievers. They believe that they are kind, intelligent, and will try different ways to communicate with their owners. They are kind and loving, but also great as companions of a child because they are tolerant. Such traits characterize the Golden Retriever and make it one of the best breeds of dogs that the canine world has to offer.

As for their ability to be trained, it's almost like the Golden Retriever knows exactly what you want them to do. These are sports dogs and hunting dogs, to be exact. Your story can tell you how this breed evolved from hunting dogs to birds until they were trained to do more. In fact, they can also carry 10 to 20 pounds of cargo, just like other large sports dogs.

But the most important thing is to know how breeders took care of their dogs. To be honest, this is not an easy task. Once you know what to consider in a good Golden Retriever breeder, and the responsibility it entails to have one, then you are ready to move on. Don't forget to build a good relationship with your dog, as this is the only thing that matters to Retrievers. Like the quoted line from the movie "Marley and I,""A dog doesn't care if you're rich or poor, educated or illiterate, smart or boring. Give him your heart, and he'll give you his."

Golden Retriever Health and Diet Tips

It is not surprising that the health of the golden retriever is based on a good and well-balanced diet, which includes proteins, fats, carbohydrates, vitamins, and minerals. Have you heard all this before about diets? Make sure you did. That's just what we are told about good diets and health for the same reasons why it is important for a dog.

Puppies should have a diet that contains a good balance of foods that contain these nutrients; otherwise, their health will suffer. It is not about feeding the puppy only food that is still more or more convenient.

Protein per puppy

The puppy's bodies develop at an alarming rate, and protein is essential to provide amino acids necessary for the maintenance and growth of strong bones and muscles. Another advantage of the protein is that it plays a key role in the production of antibodies (infection fighters) in your puppy. Protein must also be present in the puppy's body for the production and maintenance of healthy levels of enzymes and hormones.

Excellent protein food sources include eggs, meat, fish, milk, cheese, brown rice, wheat germ, and soy foods. Natural food specialists insist that eggs are actually a meal in themselves because they contain all the nutrients needed for good health.

Problems due to lack of protein

If a puppy does not get enough protein, it could actually affect his appetite because he can stop eating slowly and will have the effect that he will start losing weight, and this is certainly not what he wants in a young puppy.

Proteins play an important role in the production of antibodies, and if a puppy does not receive enough protein, it may soon begin to suffer colds and will be much more susceptible to infections and other diseases.

Protein deficiency will likely also appear in the appearance of the hair and the flaking of its gold. This will probably be one of the first signs you see in the puppy.

One sign that will help you keep in touch with your dog's health is when the coat is dull and dull. This is usually an indication of illness or ill health. When caring for a dog, the owner should always be attentive to his health to ensure that the dog does not get sick.

Although water is not a nutrient as such, a good supply of fresh water at all times is essential to a dog's health. Holding a bowl under the tap outside and filling it up is not the answer. This situation usually means that the container has algae that grow on it, which is not good for the dog at all. Water hydrates the body and transports nutrients through the body for good health.

A time to take care of giving water to a dog that stops is after a good job. Limit water consumption until the dog's breathing returns to normal. The health of the Golden retriever depends on water, especially in warm and warm climates. Dogs can sweat a lot in the warm season, and grouse dogs with their thick coat are even more affected by the heat.

Golden Retriever - Is This Breed a Good Family Dog?

They are known as purebred dogs. Unlike other breeds, the breeding of grouse dogs has just come to history only very recently. They began to evolve during the eighteenth century in Britain, thanks to Lord Tweed mouth for his immense ardor and goal to have a loyal, agile, exuberant and affectionate pet dog. He also aspired to have a dog that admires water and the ability to recover. All this marked the birth of Golden Retrievers, who possess the characteristics of being a dog beauty.

What is the purpose of double-layer skin?

Golden retriever puppies are normally double-coated and feathered in order to withstand any kind of weather, especially during cold seasons. The body is covered with straight hair, while the legs and tails have basically longer hair. Coats are more dense but soft in texture. However, during the warm seasons, the Golden retriever breed throws a lot. But this is not alarming, as is normal for your shed puppies, although heavy shedding can be minimized through proper preparation of your dog.

How is the temperament of puppies?

It is inherent in retriever puppies to possess intelligence, trust, and devotion to family members who take care of them. These puppies exude a natural charm, sweetness, and desire towards humans. However, if left alone for some time, it makes them agitated, destructive, and overly excited. However, it is innate for them to be gentle and patient with other dogs and interact very well with children and adults. Barking is your greeting to a person. Just keep in mind that this breed does not react well to being alone; they need human interaction and companionship most of the time.

How do you take care of your dog?

Proper grooming is essential for your dog. Daily brushing eliminates the heavy shedding of their coat, especially during the warm season. A solid bristle brush is available for its thick feathered layers. Use only high-quality soft shampoos.

How can you train your stray dog?

Puppy breeders find it easy to breed this type of dog. These varieties of dogs are known for their obedience, which makes them desirable drug detector trained dogs. They also have agility traits and wonderful makeup performance capabilities that make training easy and fun.

What activities are good?

They give so much pleasure and fun to be with them. Their children, rather the whole family, enjoy playing with their Golden retriever. Especially throw and retrieve balls and other types of toys. Daily exercise should be part of your activities, although sometimes you can also work out inside your home, but running outside in a safe yard from medium to large would be better.

Aspiring to have their own puppies?

Before buying a Golden retriever, make sure you understand what you should consider. Look for some of this breed and learn how to breed, feed, care, and such things. Finding a pet is as easy as you can surf the web for stray dogs for sale or ask friends who also own golden retrievers.

Golden Retriever Health Care

To enjoy your Golden Retriever for many years, it is important that you need to be aware of Golden Retriever health issues.

Not only that, but you should also always be proactive when it comes to your dog's health. Proper nutrition, exercise, and regular visits to the veterinarian will maintain the main health problems.

Consider these simple tips to guide you in caring for this breed of dog:

Veterinary Assistance

When you find a good veterinarian, you can rely on caring for your dog and can provide practical and useful medical advice regarding Golden's health problems.

A friendly veterinarian will make your dog feel safe every time he goes for his regular health checks. A visit to the veterinarian should be at least once a year.

Good preparation

Good grooming is also good health. Regular care will not only make it attractive, but it will also promote healthy skin and peeling. A regular bath and wash your coat should be a pleasant experience for your dog.

A good toilet should not be taken for granted. In fact, it should be a regular activity for you and your dog to share.

It will not only keep your dog healthy, but it will also strengthen your relationship and connection.

A good diet

A good diet is also an essential role in maintaining good health Retriever. Choose the highest quality commercial dog food to make sure it gives your dog optimal health. Always check the nutrition information on the label. You can also opt for carefully chosen human foods. Ask your veterinarian for advice on what good food you can give and what foods to avoid. With nutritious food, give your Golden Retriever plenty of water. The absence of this will lead to dehydration and other complications.

Vaccination

Vaccination is important for a good immune system of your hunting dog in order to combat common canine diseases. Your veterinarian will tell you what vaccines your dog will need.

Your Golden Retriever health care is not only for medical problems; it should also include emotional health care. Your dog is not just a creature that gives you pleasure and pleasure. He should be considered as part of the family. Give him all the love, care, and attention that will allow him to enjoy his love and affection for many years to come.

Golden Retriever Care - Tips For a Happy, Healthy Dog

Proper care Golden Retriever is essential to maintain your dog's health and happiness. Follow these simple guidelines to make sure you provide your pet with excellent care.

For a healthy puppy or young animal, Golden Retriever care is primarily about prevention and creating an environment in which your pet thrives. It is also important to monitor common health problems. These are some key factors that will help you take care of your Golden retriever properly throughout your life.

Provide the basics. The home environment of your Golden retriever should provide you with the following:

Quality food and water

A comfortable place to sleep

Toys and enough interactive playtime with you

Space for proper operation and exercise

Good grooming, brushing your teeth and bathing

Easy access to your bathroom.

Do not skip visits to the vet and look at the photos. As with all dogs, timely trips to a veterinarian and preventative strokes are essential for the proper care of the Golden retriever.

Vaccinate against Carre disease, a preventable airborne virus. Your perdiguero dog needs three injections between 6 weeks and 16 weeks for this vaccine. A booster injection is required every year thereafter.

Give your dog an annual injection to protect it from rabies, a more serious disease that is usually transmitted through the bites of animals that are already infected.

Follow all other necessary movements or reinforcements, in consultation with your veterinarian. Your veterinarian will also monitor your dog's overall health. While you may notice signs of obvious illness, your veterinarian may look for specific symptoms of treatable health problems before they become long-term.

Discover preventive medicines against filaria. Heartworms can cause problems with Circulation, Heart Failure, and sometimes death. Prevention is easier than treatment, as symptoms are often observed only in extreme cases.

Talk to your veterinarian about common Golden retriever conditions, such as hip dysplasia, and talk about how to keep your pet as healthy as possible.

Be careful. For proper care Golden retriever, you should pay attention to the physical and emotional state of your pet. Look for the following signs of Golden Retriever health problems.

Cough, vomiting, diarrhea, and fever can be signs of square disease. Take your dog to the veterinarian immediately for further diagnosis, and treatment can begin.

Diarrhea, weight loss, or biting the hind limbs can be signs of tapeworms. (Careful flea prevention can greatly help prevent tapeworms in the first place. Tapeworms and heartworms are treatable conditions, so you should check your dog immediately if you notice symptoms.

Aggression, seizures, or scum in the mouth may indicate anger. Contact your veterinarian immediately.

Unusual mood or behavior problems, signs of pain, or unusual scratching or licking may indicate health problems. Consult your veterinarian.

Good care throughout your dog's life will continue during periods of illness, and he will know that you are doing everything possible to help him. If you are attentive to the physical and emotional well-being of your pet and do not miss your visits to the veterinarian, you can provide excellent care to the Golden retriever, and you and your pet will benefit from it.

TIPS FOR QUALITY GOLDEN RETRIEVER CARE

Excellent health Golden Retriever begins with providing excellent Golden Retriever care. Here are some common ailments to keep in mind and tips for educating a healthy Golden Retriever.

For animals in full life, without pre-existing health conditions, the best step towards good health is prevention. Provide a good home environment for your pet, observe the signs of common diseases, and continue to pay attention to the physical and emotional state of your dog.

* Make sure you have provided the basics your dog will need, so you can have a happy home environment where you can thrive. Your dog needs good food, clean water, comfortable sleeping arrangements, quality toys for chewing and playing, and a lot of time and attention from you. In addition, to take good care of your

dog, you need to prepare and wet your dog properly, take care of your teeth and gums, and make sure that you do a lot of exercises. These steps will maintain Golden Retriever's good health as your dog grows and matures.

* As with all pets, do not skip visits to the veterinarian. Make sure that your dog has all the necessary and recommended vaccinations for good health. Ask your veterinarian about vaccines against Thrush, rabies, and other vaccines or booster vaccines that your dog may need. Preventive drugs against filarias is can also be administered. Your veterinarian can also monitor your dog's overall health from year to year, can give advice for good care, and can detect signs of common diseases to which your pet may be susceptible.

* Finally, pay sufficient attention to your dog's well-being. In many cases, you will be able to

find out if your pet is not feeling well. Monitor for symptoms or signs your pet is suffering and take your dog to the veterinarian immediately if you suspect he or she is sick. Symptoms to consider include weight loss, vomiting, fever, cough, diarrhea, bites or scratches, or any other unusual mood or behavior problem.

By following these simple steps, you can provide quality Golden Retriever care throughout your dog's life. Remember, for most health problems of Golden Retrievers, the sooner you take the problem, the more effective the treatment can be.

Golden Retriever Care: How to Keep Your Pet Healthy

Great health comes with giving excellent Golden Retriever care. To keep your dog happy and healthy, proper care is a must. Here is a simple guide to help you get started on the right track. Everything is a matter of prevention, especially for a puppy. This will make your pet Bloom. Educating yourself and keeping an eye on some of Goldens' common health issues are the keys.

Here are some factors that you need to keep in mind when it comes to Golden Retriever care:

1. Do not forget about the basics. An ideal home for a Golden retriever should give him the following factors:

* A beautiful, comfortable place to sleep

* Quality water and food

* Quality toys and enough time to play with family

* Good grooming, bathing, and brushing ofteeth

* Enough space for running and regular exercise

* Easy access to its " toilets."

2. Regular trips to the veterinarian. As with all breeds of dogs, regular and timely trips to veterinarians, as well as vaccinations or preventive shots are all included to ensure your pet stays healthy.

* It is important for you to give your dog annual strokes as protection against rabies, a very serious disease that can be transmitted from an infected animal to another pet.

* Consult your veterinarian if your pet needs additional boosters or shots. Your veterinarian is your partner in monitoring your dog's overall

health. You can only notice obvious symptoms of the disease, but your veterinarian may check for signs of health problems before they get worse or long-term illnesses.

* Be sure to request a vaccine against Carre disease. It is an airborne virus that is very preventable. As a rule, your pet would need three strokes within 3-16 weeks.

* Ask your veterinarian for preventive medications against heartburn. This particular condition can cause heart failure, circulation problems, and sometimes death. Symptoms of heartburn are manifested only in extreme cases, so prevention is ideal.

3. Be conscious. Proper Golden Retriever care involves being aware of the overall emotional and physical health of your pet. Be in search of the following signs:

* Vomiting, cough, and diarrhea may be signs of square's disease.

* Convulsions, aggressiveness, and foam in the mouth can be signs of anger.

* Weight loss and diarrhea may indicate tapeworms.

Pay attention to the well-being of your pet, and you will give him a wonderful beginning of a happy and long life with your family.

Golden Retriever Nutrition For Health and Energy

When considering Golden Retriever nutrition for the best care of the Golden Retriever, it is important to recognize that the Golden Retriever is a great job for dogs. Golden Retriever Dog food recipes can meet the nutritional needs of this great dog.

Proper nutrition and diet, as part of Golden Retrievers' excellent overall care, will meet dietary needs for protein, carbohydrates, fats, vitamins, and minerals. Supplements can be administered to help a dog meet daily nutritional needs. With proper nutrition and cold water, a dog will not be overweight, suffer from malnutrition, or suffer from excess or lack of minerals or vitamins.

Natural and organic ingredients are used in dog food, which can be customized. Not all natural foods are safe for a dog. Grapes, chocolate, and onions are examples of natural foods that are not safe for dogs. Cook and grind vegetables before use. Rice flour and potato flour are easily digestible. Flaxseed oil and fish oil are nutritious in dog food recipes.

Golden Retriever food recipes can be customized to meet your dog's nutritional and dietary needs. You can find Golden Retriever dog food recipes for dogs of all ages and in different health states.

Golden Retriever nutrition is essential for a good diet. Proper care of the Golden Retriever includes meeting the general nutritional needs of a dog. Golden Retriever dog food recipes are healthy.

Meat provides the easiest protein to digest. The protein provides essential amino acids for a dog's health. As for carbohydrates, ground whole grains, brown rice, potato starch, and oats can provide carbohydrates. The amount of fat consumed must be controlled. Fats help the body absorb oil-soluble nutrition. Plant fiber sources provide vitamins and minerals and enough fiber to keep the digestive tract healthy. Although beans are nutrients for dogs, beans and broccoli can cause excess gas.

When you want to develop a food plan for your dog, you should consider the amount of exercise your dog receives. A more active dog has greater nutritional needs than a sedentary dog. Extra weight occurs on a dog's body, back, hips, and joints.

For a Golden Retriever to receive the best Golden Retriever care, he must have a controlled diet that provides adequate Golden Retriever nutrition. Good Golden Retriever dog food recipes do not overfeed a Golden Retriever, who will overeat if given a chance.

You can create healthy and nutritious Golden Retriever dog food recipes from many common natural and organic food ingredients. The nutrition and dietary needs of Golden Retrievers are similar to human needs. Vegetarian diets can be modified to meet the dietary needs of dogs.

Golden Retriever nutrition is important for the overall health and happiness of a dog. If your dog needs soft food, you can find many dog food recipes to meet that need. The same applies to fat-free and wheat-free diets. You can customize the texture and size of your dog's food to meet your needs. You can create hypoallergenic diets using deer meat, lamb, fish, turkey, rice, and barley. You will also find it easy to supplement your dog's diet with oil and powder supplements that are easy to add to your dog's food.

The choice of healthy snacks such as raw carrots, natural and organic delicacies will contribute to the overall health of your dog. By providing quality chewing toys, your dog's teeth will be cleaner, and your gums will be healthy. Chewing toys can occupy a dog's attention for hours.

The proper care of Golden Retrievers requires the best foods to meet the nutritional and dietary needs of Golden Retrievers. With special attention to ingredients, their Golden Retriever dog food recipes can meet your dog's nutritional needs.

Golden Retriever - Good Hip Score

Before you start breeding Golden Retrievers, you should understand that it can be quite difficult for the breeder for the first time due to the complicated nature of breeding and other factors. In addition, success in breeding Golden Retrievers will come to you alone as long as you have a deep interest in breeding, and your knowledge in this regard is complete and complete. After all, you do not want the resulting litter to suffer because of your ignorance and lack of knowledge in breeding Golden Retrievers.

In any case, the Golden Retriever breed is not to make money quickly, and there is also an urgent need to exercise a lot of caution and do everything necessary for the proper care of the Golden Retriever who is well equipped to handle the many problems that often arise if the process is unsuccessful.

Sometimes you may have to ensure that you do not pair your dog with another dog or even with another dog of a different temperament because the litter produced by this type of breeding Golden Retrievers would give rise to different appearances, as well as provisions and therefore are not worth. In fact, proper breeding of Golden Retrievers requires doing thorough research regarding particular lines and also finding out which particular dogs will complement or even enhance the characteristics found in the dog. Therefore, it requires you to commit to doing everything necessary to ensure proper reproduction as well as be ready to provide the best in the care of Golden Retrievers once the litter has taken place.

Also note that if breeding is carried out indiscriminately, it can produce offspring that does not have the desired traits of the parents and, as a result, will lead to the distillation of the worst of the parents, which is certainly reprehensible, and not recommended at all. In addition, for those who believe that golden Retrievers education will help them earn a lot of money, they will be in great disappointment, not only because of the costs involved but also because you have to enjoy a good reputation before people buy their golden retriever puppies from you.

In general, there are many options available to the best quality breeders, and they are aware that they have to be sure to make the right decision regarding mother and father and take into account factors such as their lineage and level of intelligence, breeding, as well as age and temperament. In fact, a good reproduction of the Golden Retriever should also involve things such as the history of health problems, which must be eliminated from the next litter.

Therefore, in addition to the care of the Golden Retriever, the breeder must also perform a series of medical tests to determine the woman's medical history and then choose the male according to the results of the woman's medical tests. In fact, if you have a man who has diseases that can be transmitted genetically, then this male should be rejected by reproductive activity. In addition, it takes a long time to join the male and female, and in some cases, it may also be necessary to facilitate the Union, especially when reproductive activity is delayed.

How to Groom Your Golden Retriever

Do you take care of your dog healthy? Take these simple top grooming tips in preparation for your golden retriever care

Caring for your dog is a top program for any dog owner. Despite being a responsible dog owner, you should always have several factors to achieve this goal. Good health can be contributed by factors such as a good diet and physically should be able to undergo a good training in terms of exercise and also good obedience training. Meanwhile, in the emotional aspects, good preparation is also essential for well-being. Humans also want to play a role in their appearance through good preparation, and in this sense, animals can also have similarities. We may not know the language of the dog, but it is important that the appearance of your pets through proper preparation is sometimes molded by the actions of their owners.

As we know, different grooming tips for different breeds of dogs can provide different results. Understanding the basics of your dog is the key to grooming. Once we identify that the breed is the Golden Retriever, we will associate the type of coat with the methods for the style and groom of each of them. To begin with, your golden Cedar rooster dog is one with a beautiful thick coat. However, it has an average shedding with a soft touch and consists of a water-repellent and dense inner layer. The Golden retriever has a double layer that provides a layer of protection at any time of the year. In addition, these coats help protect them from the cold in the winter season.

Grooming the Golden Retriever is an ongoing process. The key is to bring consistency in the proper preparation of your dog. There are some common commercial toilet tricks you can take that give your Golden Retriever a great look when you leave the store. These tips can increase your dog's appearance, above all, by giving it a fresh, healthy, shiny look and inspiring a new level of confidence. Depending on the nature and type of help for the Golden retriever, the entire grooming package should be aimed at least to a minimum on the ears, eyes, fur, and nails. Preparation requires time and patience of the owner of the dog. For the love of your gold, spending at least twice a week for an hourly duration should not be a difficult task to begin with.

Tip # 1-brush your dog's coat

The process of grooming should begin with brushing the coat of the animal. Use a quality bristle brush and apply regular, regular brushing to the coat. This application, along with regular use of an undercoat rake, will seriously help reduce hair loss and can lead to a happy gold. Start the sequence from head to tail. Do not forget to brush the body and both layers for the shortest and longest length of hair to the layer. Brushing should include hair covered under the body, tail areas, the back of the legs, back, and ear areas. Remove loose hair and maintain a good inspection for your pet's body condition. Beware of skin ticks or signs of skin irritation. Fleas can be a great nuisance and easily hide under these layers, and early elimination is critical. Any form of poor hygiene should be detected early while delaying actions can lead to serious allergies and skin problems to the Golden retriever if they are not controlled.

Tip # 2-bathing your dog

The reason for bathing your dog is not only for hygienic purposes, but also helps in the prevention of fleas and ticks. This is something a Responsible Owner should do and should be adopted to reduce allergies and leaks. Golden Retrievers are naturally active animals and like to participate in the open air, while not being shy of water. These playful natures are very prone to getting dirty in the open air and potentially attract dirt, fleas, and other allergies to the street. Therefore, the owner of a dog should be sure to pay attention to maintaining a regular bath session for the dog. The water should not be too hot to burn the dog. Care should be taken so that the dog adapts to the heat. Rinse the dog with the appropriate water pressure.

The Golden Retriever Health- Common Health Problems

The health problems of the Golden Retriever are mainly congenital or hereditary. Examples of these congenital diseases are malformations in the eyes, hip dysplasia, elbow dysplasia, cancer, and even epilepsy. These common Golden Retriever health problems can be avoided by regular checkups and proper care.

Golden Retrievers ' health problems are likely to be treatable. Since most of these diseases are hereditary, it is better for a Golden Retriever owner like you to carefully monitor your pet's health. Be careful with signs and symptoms, and give your dog immediate and adequate attention. To better understand these diseases, here are the most common facts Golden Retriever health problems:

Cataract-Golden Retrievers can contract cataracts in the same way that every human can. This eye defect can be found during a routine eye checkup and can be surgically removed if the dog is healthy

Hip and elbow dysplasia: dysplasia is a debilitating disease that can cause a hip or elbow to not hold properly in its grip. This can lead to degenerative joint disease that causes more pain and limits the mobility of the Golden Retriever. If left unattended, this disease can develop into arthritis later in life.

Arthritis: arthritis affects Golden Retrievers in the same way it affects humans. This disease makes it difficult for your pet to move and can be treated with injectable painkillers. It can be administered at home or at any veterinary clinic. Giving your pet a warm bath is also a good way to relieve pain in their joints.

Cancer-Golden Retrievers often face blood cancer and cancer of the lymphatic system. Unfortunately, there is no cure for this disease. Both conventional and homeopathic remedies can be used depending on what you think is best for your dog.

Epilepsy: this is a disorder of the brain that can cause a concussion or periodic seizures. This condition can usually be controlled with appropriate medications.

Prevention is better than cure. The best way to prevent these health problems is to examine dogs before mating properly. To be sure, you can ask your breeder to produce the necessary documents and even provide an X-ray result. The most recognized breeders update the documents and X-ray recordings of their dux every 18 months. As part of your overall Golden Retriever care, serving your gold with the right food is the best way to prevent and combat these diseases. A regular trip to your veterinarian, immediate treatment, and appropriate medications can almost certainly put the Golden Retriever health problems away.

Maintenance of The Golden Retriever Puppy

These are the most tender puppies

You shouldn't buy a Golden retriever puppy just because you think it's the cutest puppy you've ever seen. You buy this pet to be your family pet for life, not just for a few weeks. Let "all puppies be cute" be your mantra during the process of searching for your puppy.

New Golden Retriever care

Puppies of Golden Retrievers are not much different from any other puppy. Prevention is better, so maintenance and general checks on well - being are important. Start by choosing a responsible breeder who will already have a game plan for your puppy's health put in place; just follow it.

Preparation is another part of your Golden retriever puppy's care to consider; although they are not as demanding as some breeds, they require a regular preparation routine. Set up a schedule for daily activities involving your puppy. Brushing at a certain time every day and bathing the same day every week should make your golden retriever easy to handle.

How to find puppies for sale

Start by finding the breeder you can trust, not the puppy you like. If the breeder considers it better not to have a puppy, it is worth waiting for a little.

But if you do not want to wait, you can consider shops, newspapers, or the internet to buy golden retriever puppies. Prices may seem cheaper and may seem even more tempting because they are available now, but try to prevent the momentum. But there is a risk that the adult dog does not have all the attributes of temperament that he liked about the breed.

Name your new Golden Retriever puppy

Remember that the name is for life, not only for the time of the puppy, and practical aspects should also be considered. The name should be easy to remember for your dog, not offensive to other owners, and suggestive to your expectations.

You can choose a name that means something to you, or you can be inspired by pop culture, classic animal names, or the internet. Choose a name for a male and a female would be advisable, as some breeders will not allow you to choose the puppy for you, as they are often a better judge of which puppy would suit you and your needs with your interview.

The right Golden Retriever puppy will choose the right owner

The search for the perfect golden retriever puppy can take up to a month or more, depending on the region in which it lives. It is worth taking your time to work with a breeder who can provide you with the puppy that has the temperament and physical attributes you are looking for and are waiting for your future adult dog. Feel free to buy the first puppy you see or like and remember that all the puppies are cute, but the right one for you and your family is waiting, and you will find yourself. And do not forget that you are ready to take care of the puppy you will buy, with the necessary information and things, because from the moment you left the dog breeder, the puppy is your responsibility.

Your Pet Golden Retriever Deserves the Best in Care & Feeding

Learn the best ways to feed and care for your Golden Retriever pet

Why Golden Retrievers are relatively large dogs, most people consider them outdoor dogs. Although it works well if you have a construction site, it is not if you live in an apartment or condominium. Golden Retriever loves to be around people and interact with them, but sometimes they like to have their privacy. Outdoor dogs will probably have their own home, while the indoor pet will have more trouble finding a private place.

The way to solve this problem is to train your golden retriever dog in cash. After training your pet to go to his box to be alone, when he needs to leave or have guests, you can connect the animal without problems. Do not use the box to punish the animal, but reward it when training them to use it. Put your favorite toys and bedding in the box so that they feel comfortable. Over time, it will be the place of refuge of your pet that could disturb you. If you live in a harsh climate, it may be good to have a covered place as well as its exterior.

Frequent care is a must for your Golden retriever pet, especially if they come into the house. They have a double layer and a shed all year round. Their inner layer is thick and helps protect them from the cold. When the winter is over, start pulling this coat, so it's good practice to brush every day.

Approximately every two weeks, you need the groom and bathe your pet to keep their fur and skin healthy. Start by brushing anywhere while checking for fleas, ticks, and other skin problems. At the same time, check the ears of your pet and cut the nails. Unlike many dogs, your Golden retriever dog will love being wet. Use only dog shampoo because human shampoo will dry your pet's skin. If possible, you should use a natural type of dog shampoo.

Feeding the food of your golden house would be the ideal situation. It does not take long when following a recipe. The cost is usually no more than you have to pay for a premium dog food. Choose recipes that characterize different meats and vegetables so that your pet does not get tired of them. If you can not prepare homemade food for your pet, buy the best you can afford. Make sure it does not contain artificial ingredients or cereal fillings.

We recommend that you have a program to feed your Golden Retriever puppy. It should be three times a day for 20 minutes at a time. If you do not eat all the food at that time, remove the container. It will not be long before they realize that they need to eat all the food. At this time, you can start increasing the amount of food. After 12-20 weeks, take the same amount of food and divide it into two servings per day. Twice a day, feedings are recommended for the rest of their lives.

Here is an easy way to understand how much you should feed your golden adult pet every day. Take your body weight and multiply it by 0.4. This number will correspond to the total amount of ounces of food that your pet should eat in a day.

No more feeding your golden retriever pet. If you can't feel their ribs without hitting them, they're probably heavy. If you are working on animals instead of dogs, be sure to exercise a lot. If you do not have a large area for them to find themselves trying to find a dog park or somewhere, you can leave them without the leash.

Always have clean and freshwater for them. Make sure that your bowl is always full. If they are indoor and outdoor dogs, it is a good idea to have two sources of water. A dog door will make it easier for them to reach another source when it is dry. It's also a great thing to have if you like to go on the patio very well, especially at night.

Caring for your pet Golden retriever is not so difficult, as they are not really so picky from where they live. However, you should make it as comfortable as possible. Make sure they have a private place. Try to feed your pet with natural homemade food, if possible, but if you can not get the best you can afford. Make sure they always have freshwater. Do these things for your pet, and they will reward you by becoming your best friend.

Understanding Golden Retriever's Allergies So You Care Better For Them

It's good when they say that a dog carries a whole load of responsibility. You need to be careful to keep a dog very healthy and beautiful. Unfortunately, there are many reasons that can cause various golden retriever allergies that can make your dog extraordinarily uncomfortable.

Golden Retrievers are certainly prone to many skin allergies that could lead to vital health problems if left untreated. There may be several reasons why they have such types of infection, intervention, parasites, and other allergies.

There are four main types of Golden Retrievers allergies to consider:

Allergy to fleas

Food Allergies

Atopy

Contact allergy

Flea allergy: this is usually the skin infection that could occur due to an allergic reaction of saliva to fleas. If it is the allergy that your dog is going through, the first thing you may notice in your body is a small red papule, which will slowly turn into a crust. These types of Golden Retrievers allergies are commonly affected in the lower back, thighs, belly, hind legs, and hind legs. Flea infection is one of the most common Golden Retriever allergies when you find your dog excessively itchy and scratched.

Food Allergies: sometimes, a Golden retriever may have food allergies. Foods such as wheat, beef, dairy products, and soy could be the reasons for this type of food allergy. The only way to be sure that your dog is going through a food allergy is to change its diet completely. When changing your diet, be sure to give yourself a sufficient amount of vitamins and nutrients. This diet should be continued up to eight weeks without interruption and observe the results.

Atopy: this type of golden retriever allergy occurs when the dog reacts to certain substances or inhales something that could cause this reaction. This type of allergy causes the dog to scratch excessively and affected areas in areas such as feet, face, underarms, and groin. If this is not treated, it can cause the thickening of the infected area with a serious infection. Some common substances to which Golden Retrievers are allergic are pollen, fungal spores, weeds, cat hair, and certain types of grass.

Contact allergy: this is the least common of all allergies because dogs always have a protective layer on their body. But when a dog suffers from some kind of other allergies, it could add to the affected area. Substances such as enamels, waxes, and chemicals for carpet washing are some examples.

Dogs are like humans in many of their reactions and need a lot of care and attention from their owners. Owners need to be attentive, and the sooner a problem is solved, the better. Golden retriever allergies are a serious problem, and if left untreated, they could cause life-threatening circumstances.

How to Take Care of a Black Golden Retriever

Say that you have a litter of puppies, and during cleaning, notice that something is not quite correct with any of them. You can hardly believe what he sees, but in the middle of his butter-colored brothers, there is a black puppy that mixes blindly.

Now you should not worry at all. The Black Gold Perdiguero dog, as most dog lovers theorize, is simply a very rare and recessive gene that has been expressed by the puppy. Most enthusiasts trace the origin of this gene to one of the ancestors of the Golden, the flat-haired retriever. This type of retriever had a black coat gene in its genetic composition, and it is possible that this gene is simply buried in the depths of modern Partridge dogs. However, this shows that the black Golden grouse dog is no different from those of golden color and does not need special attention or treatment.

For the most part, caring for Black Goldens is almost the same as caring for gilts. They will mature and grow at the same rate, which means they need the same amount of food. For puppies under three years old, you need to feed them three times a day. Mature dogs need to eat only once a day, unless the dog exercises regularly, it can feed it twice. You will need to refer to a specific age for race, weight, and height to know how to feed your little black bundle of joy properly.

Another similarity between the two "varieties" is that they are both very intelligent. Puppies are curious and like to explore and are ready to learn new things. If you try to teach Black Gold tricks or try to train it in the bathroom, you will find that it is usually not easier or more difficult to do. You can use the same methods, tips, and strategies you use to train a white or Golden grouse dog. You can teach both types of stray dogs to walk with a leash and a collar or harness without problems.

Since your biggest difference is the color of your coat, it is possible that this is what would be different in your care. For white or Golden grouse dogs, it is easy to brush and check the skin and the underlying skin when the skin is light, and the skin is easy to detect under the skin. For the Black version, however, since the fur is black and it is more difficult to detect parasites such as fleas and ticks that hide in the fur. Then you can use several repellent fleas or ticks on a black grouse dog.

So, as you can see, apart from the color difference of the dress, the two partridges are similar to each other. As long as you have the same patience and passion for launching your black golden retriever as for the Golden retriever, then you will have no problem taking care of this beautiful black baby!

The Love, Training, Obedience, and care

The Golden Retriever, with its intelligence and eager attitude to please, is one of the most popular breeds in the United States according to AKC registration statistics. The working capacity that made the Golden Retriever such a useful hunting companion also makes it an ideal dog for guidance, assistance, and search and rescue. The golden coat is the hallmark of this versatile breed and can range from light gold to dark gold.

The Golden Retriever is an adorable, well educated, intelligent dog with great charm. These dogs are easily trained, and always patient and friendly to children. They are faithful, confident, gentle, and eager to please. It is an active, loving, and outstanding family dog. Golden Retrievers like to please their teachers so that obedience training can be fun.

They excel in obedience competitions. Friendly to everyone, including other dogs, the Golden Retriever has very little, if any, surveillance instincts. Although it is unlikely to attack, Goldens makes good guard dogs, pointing out aloud the approach of a stranger.

You should make sure to keep this dog firm, but quiet and safe, consistent pack leader behavior to avoid behavioral problems. Some of Golden's talents are hunting, tracking, recovery, drug detection, agility, competitive obedience, and trick execution. These dogs also like to swim.

All these attributes of the Golden Retriever make it one of the most sought after dogs. It's a pleasure to have one of these absolutely beautiful dogs. A companion you will appreciate by your side on walks and a pleasant companion on those cold and rainy days, you will only be inside.

Golden Retriever Training

Owning a golden retriever puppy is a lot of fun for everyone, but it is important that the plush ball begins with basic puppy training as soon as possible. Teaching a new puppy the basic commands is better because they can't learn much when it's really small, but some commands will bring some sort of order into their life. As the puppy grows, more training can be implemented.

When training a puppy, the idea is to use a command from a word and show the puppy what it means by hand movements. Puppies have very short attention stretches, so long workouts will benefit neither the puppy nor the owner. Several sessions of 10 minutes a day, in order to achieve the best results. Do not forget about these delights when the puppy has the right thing;he will want some kind of reward.

You may wonder why to train a puppy, but the fact is that if a puppy can get away with bad habits when he is young, it will be much more difficult to train later. It is better to immediately start the puppy from the right foot, and everyone will be happy. In fact, dogs can be quite bored to treat if they have a lot of bad behavior habits. One of those behaviors I insisted on changing is the mockery of the food while trying to put the food in the bowl (assuming the bowl is on the ground or the ground!). I've always had my dogs sit next to the bowl and wait until I say "eat " before they can start eating. It was much cleaner and better organized, especially if you have more than one animal.

Basic commands

These commands are " Sit, Stay, come. "There is not much? As mentioned above, these commands are used as single-word commands. It will not work if you are given a command like "stop running on the road, Goldie."There are too many words for the dog to understand.

It's a good idea to use the dog's name first, then the command. When the puppy receives an order in this way, if there are other dogs around (or even small children for that matter), the puppy will know, how he gets to know his name, and what the order is for him. Say, "Goldie. Sit. "Goldie. Stay. "Goldie. Be." Use the name of the dogs, pause, and then command.

Training should begin with the use of the puppy's name from the very beginning. Then the command should not be: "puppy, come on. "It's a good idea to use the puppy name, as much as possible, until you see it start taking note when you use it.

As smart as dogs are, this is the sound they get used to. Do you think when you say a dog, you know what you say in your sunburn? No, but what we notice is the fact that your voice has changed, and you can say that you are not happy.

Use a firm voice when training a puppy so that he can recognize that he is referring to business by giving him a command. A lot of praise and a lot of love will go a long way with the formation of a golden retriever puppy.

What to Expect from a Leading Golden Retriever Training Manual

The adoption of a Golden retriever comes with serious commitments in terms of time, care, and health. If you've never had a pet before, it's a good idea to talk to some dog owners and find out what time and money it takes to be a Golden Retriever parent. When you decide to be a Golden retriever puppy parent, it is a good idea to get a Golden retriever Leader Training Guide to give you information about training, feeding, health, caring, and exercise to take care of your new arrival.

Dogs can become the most faithful of companions when they are well treated, and many owners say they are more faithful than humans, and I have to say from experience that I have discovered that this is the case. If your dog is treated the right way, it will be your protector, your constant companion, and a comforter.

Have you ever experienced the absolute loyalty of a dog when you were sick? My husband had a hip replacement, and for six weeks of recovery after the operation, our dog, Trixie, just walked away. When my husband suffered, the dog would sit with his head on his knees, and he (the dog!) would have sadder eyes. I could even tell when my husband was suffering just by watching Trixie.

Total care of your dog.

Proper dog care requires more than food and water. "Just food and water" means you put food and a bowl of water somewhere that the dog can drink, but really taking care of a dog goes much further. The diet should be quality food that will give the dog all the nutrients it needs for a good strong bone and healthy muscles, and the water should be clean and fresh every day. Bowls should be cleaned daily to remove bacteria that can cause infection. Busy owners sometimes feel that it is a burden to clean the dog's Bowls, but it is inhumane not to clean them and even more expensive if the dog gets sick.

Raising a puppy should be even more careful with his diet and general education. The first years of the life of a puppy see him grow rapidly, develop growing bones and muscles. A puppy needs to receive the right vitamins for muscle growth and for his bones to become beautiful and strong.

All this information can be obtained from the main training manuals of golden retrievers, as they are written specifically for this breed of dog.

Golden Retrievers need to have the time given to their grooming as well because they have a long coat that needs to be brushed at least once a week and more often during the detachment season. In addition, they need regular cleaning of the feet, nails, ears, eyes, and other areas that may be troubling.

Exercise is also an important element of the care of a Golden retriever puppy or an adult dog. They need exercise to keep the muscles strong, and exercise is also necessary to keep them in a healthy mental state. Golden Retrievers especially need exercise because they were bred to be a hunting dog and need to have a good long period on a regular basis. They are very smart dogs, and if they do not exercise and receive games to play soon, they will suffer emotionally and physically.

A golden retriever Leader Training Manual will cover puppy steps into adulthood, and really any dedicated owner will want to do everything they can for their dog and learn everything they can about the breed and how to take care of their chosen puppy.

Tips for Brushing your Golden Retriever

Get ready to brush your thick gold. Remember that one thing; All Golden Retrievers do is pour. There is absolutely no way to avoid it.

Brushing is a way to keep some of your hair in your clothes and furniture, but more than that, this very basic activity keeps your coat clean, tangle-free, and, most importantly, shiny. You want to practice at least once a week and sometimes twice a week.

It is also very important for brushing. It stimulates your circulation and helps maintain healthy skin.

Even with this seemingly simple act, there is an accurate way to brush a Golden Retriever.

Before touching a brush for your dog's hair, lightly spray your dog's coat with water. Some golden parents prefer to spritz with a diluted conditioner. Simply mix a tablespoon of balm to 16 ounces of water in a spray bottle.

The conditioner helps prevent static electricity and hair breakage. Once you have sprayed your coat, brush or comb your hair in the direction, they naturally grow.

When you get an area where the hair is longer than the other parts of the body, such as the tail, the back of the legs, the back, and behind the ears, simply divide the hair into sections. Brush or paint each of these sections separately and smooth the sections again.

Make sure the powder on your skin. This prevents the carpet. However, do not put too much pressure on your skin. This is especially true if the brush uses metal tips that can scratch.

Simple Steps to Follow when Training Yourself

The Golden Retriever was raised around 1800 in Britain, with the aim of recovering the game. Golden retriever puppy training was already endemic at that time that dogs use for both recovery and hunting. Today, Golden Retrievers are considered to serve a variety of purposes to their owners: guide dogs, guard dogs, companion dogs, service dogs, and field trials.

The Golden Retriever is best described as friendly and cheerful. This type of dog is eager to make its owners happy at all times, and training is usually simple. They like to be with other animals and children. Their friendly nature makes them the perfect family pet. While they normally love everyone, they are vigilant of their owners when strangers are around.

They have almost an unlimited supply of energy, so the activities that are perfect for them are the type of endurance activity. If left alone for a while or separated from family members, Retrievers can become annoying or destructive. These dogs are at their best if they are equipped with tasks to perform, such as recovery, hunting, or performing activities that will involve their ability to think intelligently. Golden Retrievers are excellent swimmers and dock riders, so there's a good chance they'll jump into the water when you're away from it.

To ensure proper training of the puppy, start taking them to active exercises from 2 months with the following:

1. Daily routine: Teach and train puppies to take their food and water dishes from where they are, how often and at what time of day they need to eat (morning, afternoon and night),

where their bed and bath is, where they kept their toys, and what routes to take to walk or run around the world.

2. Proofreading: Teach the Golden Retrievers what the word "no" means and what they should stop doing when they hear the word.

3. Words of praise: Words of praise makes them feel good. Recognize good works and let them know that the word "good" is a form of recognition.

4. Cash formation: These would probably be the cornerstone of your future Jump and active training.

5. Break: You should immediately present it in your bathing place, but a 2-3-month-old puppy is still a baby, so it will be several months before your internal organs are sufficiently developed for reliability.

6. Acceptance to manage it. Puppies must also be trained to follow the rules and agree to follow the owner's orders. But love and care must also be included, as always.

7. Softness: Teaching him the meaning of the word "simple" does not mean biting or calm.

After celebrating its third month, it's time for more advanced training.

Teach you to:

1. Lie

2. Lie down for up to 30 minutes

3. Look straight at your house when you say his name

4. Recognize his name and see you as you call him

5. Teach him to be patient and wait outside the door until he is allowed in

6. Walking on a leash without pulling

7. Stop barking when you say, " calm down."

8. Politely interact with strangers and other animals

9. Give up everything that is in your mouth with the words "give" or " let go."

Training Golden Retriever puppies, like any other teaching experience, would require a lot of patience and effort.

Potty Training a Golden Retriever Puppy is a Serious Business

Pet care has great responsibilities. Includes food, training, and toilets. And this is true for all kinds of animals. But for the most common pet that is considered man's best friend, training is a big responsibility. That is why it is recommended to encourage yourself at a certain age just to care for dogs. A popular breed of dog that many American families keep as a pet is Golden Retriever. Potty training a golden retriever puppy is really one of the first training programs that every pet owner should consider; otherwise, they will probably end up hating their pet.

As soon as you take your puppy home, you should immediately take it to the designated place where you want it to turn into a pot. Why is that? There are two main reasons for this.

The first is that you want to present it immediately in this place, you will probably feel it and get to know it. Second, the journey where you come from may be long enough for you to want to urinate. Remember that puppies under six months of age cannot control the bladder for more than six hours.

This is also the reason why it is necessary to establish a regular routine to impregnate a puppy. As far as possible, if you belong to a large family with children who have agreed to take care of your new pet, include them in the program. In this way, children are not only trained to be responsible for training to go to the toilet of the new puppy but also to bond with their new friend. Golden Retrievers are well known for having a happy and friendly personality. Therefore, it is better if each family member has the opportunity to take him to walk and play with him regularly.

I remember my friend, who adopted a Golden retriever. He has three children: the eldest is 17 years old, the second is 15 years old, and the youngest is 13 years old. In fact, he made a decree for the three children to alternate in the invasive training of their puppy. He brought all three together, and they all created a program that everyone will respect. And then, they published a place where everyone can consult, so there's no excuse to miss their show.

Another important reminder about a puppy's pots is in the event that he accidentally urinates or makes a mess inside the house does not stick or hurt his dog. Remember that they do not have complete control of the situation. Damaging them could only lead your dog to develop unpleasant behaviors.

Remember all these tips for invading a puppy, and you will be sure of a happier and safer pet. After all, the potty is one of the essential training courses you can get.

Golden Retriever Adoption

So, you want to have a golden Retriever adoption? Instead of buying one in a pet store, the idea of adopting one in a shelter is much better. Not only will it save a lot of money, but it will also save a life when you adopt one. Although it is better to adopt an adult Golden retriever, the adoption of a puppy will be more useful. Seeing a puppy grow up in your loving care would make you feel more blessed. Historically grown up as gun dogs with a sweet mouth, the Golden retriever also has a sweetheart.

The friendly and warm behavior of the Golden Retriever makes it the fourth most popular family dog breed in the United States. The intelligence and versatility of the breed are very suitable for dogs for a variety of roles, companion, guide dog for the blind, hunting dog, illegal drug detector, fire, and search and rescue dog. This is one of the breeds of Dogs of high rank in terms of intelligence, agility, and obedience. To adopt and care for a golden retriever puppy would not be a problem, even if you are the owner of a dog for the first time.

Any puppy adoption should be well studied first. You need to make sure that this dog is the breed that best suits your personality. Friendly, kind, and faithful dogs require their owners to be active and love to be on the move as they do. They have high energy levels and love to run and evacuate. They are also very young for a long time, about four or five years.

So, if you want to have a bright young companion long enough, then the Golden retriever is definitely for you. When considering adoption, remember that dogs are working, and therefore, have to work all the time. They always want to have something in their mouth, so it would be a good idea to provide them with a lot of chew toys. They are very social dogs and want to be with people most of the time.

They should have obedience training as soon as possible. And most importantly, do not calm down until you have completely passed the puppy stage. It is best to take note of these facts if you want to have this type of dog for a pet. Also, they do not make good house dogs. The ideal environment to live in a house with a large garden, and the ideal family to own this type of dog would be a family with children of school age.

When you have decided that the Golden retriever is the most suitable dog breed for you and your family, go to the animal shelter or the closest human society to you and choose your dog. And it is better to know the needs of your puppy. Find out why it was registered and placed in the shelter.

Knowing the history of the puppy will help you to properly care for it, which makes you a good pet owner. Comply with all regulations before adopting a Golden retriever. And give him a dog tag and a leash. Always obey all the laws of the leash and be sure to take water for swimming from time to time. Adapt to the personality of your puppy and always try to understand his needs.

Adopt a Golden Retriever Puppy and Get a Friend for Life

Are you single and looking for a partner, but do not want to enter into a relationship? Have you experienced any kind of melancholy lately and want to recover? Well, this might be the right solution for you. Do you know that when you adopt a golden retriever puppy, you will definitely benefit? Although I must warn you so early that caring for a golden retriever is a serious commitment, it is also good to keep in mind that it can benefit your overall well-being.

Goldens are well known for their beautiful, loving, and friendly personality. They are also an intelligent breed of dogs, so they are mainly trained for hunting. They are native to Scotland, where they were used for hunting and also trained as a working dog on the farm, and you can be sure that they can also be a very gentle and affectionate pet for you. But just like a word of caution, however, they may not be the best guard for your home because they can easily make friends with strangers.

Now let's go back to the previous step that I painted. I said that if you're feeling a little depressed lately because you broke up with your longtime partner, you might consider adopting a golden retriever puppy. You certainly don't need to worry about having a relationship while you're on the rebound, but you can also consider the amount of time you need to spend taking care of your new puppy.

There are several must-do that you need to consider before adopting a golden retriever puppy. I will share with you some of these care tips that will surely make your new Golden Retriever happy.

Nutrition is an important component of the care of your new pet. Adopting a golden retriever puppy, you need to know what is the best type of diet you need to provide. Do you know that, like children, they will need all the necessary nutrients to help them develop their bones and muscles? The power frequency is a piece of additional information to keep in mind. Since they are a child growing up alone, you should feed them regularly according to a schedule.

Training is another important lesson to learn in caring for your Goldens. By training them into the dogs you want them to become, you are not only creating a disciplined dog but also doing yourself a favor. You do not have to worry that your puppy spoils so much, and you will also make him a happy dog around your friends.

Exercise is another reminder. This is where you will probably enjoy it. Since your newly adopted puppy requires regular exercise, in the form of walking, playing, and even swimming, you will be forced to get up and stay with your dog. Surely, you do not want strangers to walk with your dog, or you will eventually lose a new friend.

Common Golden Retriever Health Issues

You Should be Aware of Before Adopting

When looking for a Golden Retriever puppy, it is better to visit a breeder. Be well prepared, read about Golden Retriever, and know when to ask questions and what to ask. Ask about your condition, if you have heart problems or concerns with critical parts of your body. Skin irritations and diseases are a concern for the health of perverted dogs.

Let a veterinarian check immediately for any signs of uneven skin color, blemishes, or pain. A good and reliable breeder will be open and honest enough to answer the questions posed. They should be able to provide the necessary information and solutions, if necessary.

These wonderful puppies come from England and Scotland, from where they got their affectionate character, kindness, and pleasure. People appreciate your company and friendship. Taking care of their health by giving them quality food plus exercise will definitely give them a life to enjoy.

One thing to keep in mind about the health of Golden Retrievers is that there are health conditions in most of them. Therefore, it is essential to get a puppy from a well-known high-quality dog breeder. As far as possible, bring the puppies while they are still young. The younger, the better so that they can have the best possible control of health. In addition, provide them with the right diet, proper exercise, and visits to veterinarians. Preventive medicine is better than cure, as it will keep them away from the common health problems that groupers are prone to.

Here are some of these common health problems observed in this type of breed:

Hip dysplasia

One of the most common health problems of Golden Retrievers is hip dysplasia. Hip dysplasia is a common disease. It's genetic and related to arthritis. They tend to accumulate crystals in the articular cartilage that lead to arthritis, and this problem has spread from this point. Caution is advised, as it sometimes affects your muscles, and when this happens, they may become motionless.

Not being able to move makes a Retriever depressed. It is not possible to predict all cases of hip dysplasia. At this stage of the disease, it is strongly recommended to consult a specialist doctor. And it is also advisable not to administer medicines without a prescription.

Von Willebrand disease

Von Willebrand's disease is a hereditary clotting disorder. This disease is very complex and has something to do with the blood clotting factor. Some canine medical experts suggest that asking vet Von Willebrand right away is a necessity, as blood platelets tend to accumulate inappropriately. This will lead to easy and prolonged bleeding.

Eye defects

The Golden Retriever also has congenital malformations in the eyes at an early age. A hereditary cataract is also one of the common eye problems for this breed. In addition, they are also prone to ARPC or so-called "Central progressive retinal atrophy."This affects the reception of light in the dog's eye. Difficulties with night vision and poor lighting are the main manifestations of this disease

Poor quality commercial food is not good for the health of the Golden Retriever and also for almost all other dogs. Not only should you be careful about what feeds your dogs, but you should also consider the amount and be careful not to overfeed them. Soy products are not recommended for Golden Retrievers.

Breeding Golden Retrievers is Something Special

One of the most difficult tasks as the owner of the animal is dog breeding. This type of activity, especially the breeding of Golden Retrievers, involves a very complex activity. There are many considerations and requirements set out in the breeding of Golden retriever dogs. These criteria must be met to ensure their quality and health.

First of all, the history of the dog is considered highly. These breeds are prone to congenital diseases that are usually transmitted from parents to children. That's why most breeders are very meticulous. They must do everything possible to ensure the health and safety of their careers.

Secondly, breeders make sure that the genes of the dog are not aligned with diseases. It willbe a bad sign for your business if most of your dogs have bad genes.

In addition to tracking dog genes from parents to offspring, there are still other things they do to make sure they breed Golden retriever as high-quality dogs.

Not only is your time and effort spent on dog care, but it can also be very expensive. Especially the care and breeding of female golden dogs. When a bitch is pregnant, everything doubles, care, effort, and money. Bitches are too risky. They must be in the right process to give birth to healthy puppies. Attention is very necessary for Golden retriever women. If dogs do not receive proper care and attention, it is possible that these dogs will no longer breed.

Many medical examinations need to be carried out to ensure the quality of the dogs. The story must be traced correctly to show if the Golden retriever has no signs of illness. Breeding Golden Retrievers can be very expensive. Medical testing is one of the main tasks of breeders. They make sure the price of the dog is in line with the health of the dog.

Golden retriever breeding is something you need to stay focused on. From the care and money spent on caring for and growing them, we can not ask ourselves as animal owners why these breeds are so expensive. Breeders assured that the work that was given to the dogs. They assured the dogs are in good condition. The history and generation of dogs have also been monitored to ensure that any buyer gets the right dog.

Breeding Golden Retrievers is also fun, although despite the expenses and efforts. This is because these dogs are very adorable and playful. They have these traits to make their owners happy and happy with their presence. They look forward to having fun and playing. Definitely, because it would be the best dog in the family, as a pet owner, you would enjoy every time you walk with your dog.

Such a price for having this kind of dog. Just make sure that the breeding process makes your investment worthwhile. If you are going to buy golden puppies, always consult with the parents. If you are going to buy dog gold, be sure to review and have a copy of your medical tests and document history. This is the best way to make sure you have the right and healthy dog at home.

Research the breed Before you Buy

Are you considering buying a Golden retriever as an addition to your family? You made the right choice! It is the breed that is most appreciated in the country. Golden Retrievers are perfect complete family dogs thanks to their intelligence, patience, and loyalty. You should look for the breeder before buying a golden retriever. There are certain things that need to be taken into account.

The first step would be to prepare together with your own family, allowing them to learn more about the Golden Retriever breed. You may have had such a breed before, or we are aware of them. So it would be good preparation for another animal. If you've never had a dog before, you can search for the breed before buying a Golden retriever by reading this topic as well as on how to take care of it. This will prepare one for the new addition to the family. It will also make me very confident when it comes to taking care of the dog. You do not need to limit your search to Golden Retriever. Before you go to check the puppies, you need to do a background check on the organization of where you get the dog. It is best not to see the puppies before doing this or that you might be hit by a cute puppy.

We need to be sure that you get your puppy from a famous breeder. Most pet stores claim to get their dogs from reputable breeders, but the fact is that they only order dogs from some puppy factories. Establishments that breed dogs are usually in scary conditions. They do not pay attention to congenital malformations that can worsen due to reckless reproduction. Puppy mills dogs have a high probability of suffering from chronic health problems throughout life. A responsible breeder will take care of raising only dogs that do not have health problems because the same could be passed on to puppies. It is always better to look for the breed before buying Golden retriever. It makes you the fact that good breeders have documents that provide detailed information about their dogs. You get to know the meaning of your puppy. You may also be able to see the dam and father so you have an idea of what your puppy will look like once he grows up. You can also adopt a puppy from an organization that saves Golden Retriever. These dogs are usually abandoned due to circumstances beyond their control. Otherwise, these are perfect breed dogs.

When you decide to go see the puppy, you should try to spend time with her. You also need to take with you the members of their family with whom the dog will live. Everyone should be able to get along with it as well as others around. This should be done so that all family members are ready to have a dog in the house. Even if a member is not passionate, this could lead to the ruin of the careful training that has been done, if that member does not participate in the care of the dog. Look for the breed before buying Golden retriever so that you have no regrets after.

What to Look for in a Golden Retriever Breeder

There are many Golden retriever breeders all over the world, to name a few, we have the Rusty Golden Retriever breeder, European Cedar Rooster dogs, and many more. Once you are endowed with much of the knowledge of having puppy Partridge dogs at home, you cannot deny yourself and resist the desire to want to have one for your family. Having them around is quite amazing and involves a warm and safe society for you and your family.

But choosing and selecting your puppy through its appearance is not enough. It is essential that we also consider how they have been raised. Even if you know all the basic facts about retriever puppies, it is always appropriate to know more in the context of the dog or puppy you want to buy.

The choice of the best breeder Golden Retriever will ensure the quality of the breeds of these dogs. When you say the best, these breeders are qualified for their time; spend, and focus on quality time to raise exceptionally healthy and well-trained dogs.

However, it should not depend entirely on breeders. It is also recommended to do homework, read and study more about the dog perdiguero. Try to get acquainted with the important factors of this breed, such as care, temperament, illness, the importance of their coats, nutrition, training, exercise, and other important facts available.

Although it is innate that they are obedient, it is not good to be informed at random, since there are also important details that you should learn to avoid breeding destructive and lush dogs. Don't be too lax as you naturally learn what you read online about them. Increase the needs of your patience, time, and work. But all this is nothing compared to what your well-trained golden retriever breed can give you. It is extremely rewarding and satisfying.

With little attention to the reproduction, problems usually arise. Although they are a healthy breed, it is inevitable that they are also susceptible to the disease. The most common diseases are hip dysplasia and cataracts. A cataract is usually transmitted genetically from parents to their offspring. I recommend that before you buy your goldfish in a pet store or a golden retriever breeder, take a look. You can ask the OFA or the Orthopedic Foundation to check your dog. They provide X-rays and other tests to check the good health of their puppies or dogs in this matter.

Another way to get to know your Golden retriever is to get to know the personality of the Breeders. If they are good, they can attract or bring excellent dogs even when good breeders take care of their pets.

Be patient and take the time to look for a brilliant breeder. Anyway, this will guarantee you puppies of remarkable quality.

With perseverance in the search for an exemplary qualified golden retriever breeder, you and your family will spend a joyful and wonderful time with your dog. They are an excellent companion, provide absolute security in your home, and will certainly give you a fun and loving aura in your home. They are tender and affectionate.

Golden Retriever Food: Feeding Your Dog Human Food

Golden Retriever food should always be carefully chosen in order to give your dog a nutritious and delicious meal. Sometimes owners take shortcuts when it comes to their dog's food. Any dog food for sale in the supermarket is bought and fed to the animal without checking the nutritional value. If you really care about the health of your Golden Retriever, you can skip the hallway for now and check your refrigerator. You may be surprised to find that what is good for you may be good for him.

Get rid of what you learned about myths about human food like Golden Retriever food. Your dog would also prefer variety in their dish, and giving them carefully selected human food would make them love more.

Meats like chicken and turkey are good food. You can combine them with raw vegetables or cut fruits. Although human foods, their nutritional value is beneficial to your dog.

Other nutritious human food choices for your retriever are:

* Raw eggs/egg yolk including its shells-rich in protein.

* Raw vegetables: carrots are the best

* Brown rice is rich in fiber; good for you and your retriever.

* Oatmeal - also rich in fiber

* Fruit-skip grapes and raisins; give your golden retrievers apples, peaches, or bananas, to name a few.

You should avoid giving the following human food to your dog retriever:

* Chocolates-a bromine that leads to toxicity in your dog. Unsweetened chocolates contain the greatest amount of bromine.

* Egg whites - can cause biotin deficiency (Vitamin B) because of this contains avid in, but you can give your retriever a whole raw egg, including the eggshell.

* Onions and garlic

Most human foods are perfect for your dog, but there are some that are not and can also harm your dog. It can also be a source of skin allergies or may even cause instant death.

It is always good to mix human food with your dog's croquette. Always keep in mind, even if raw and cooked food is a complete and balanced diet, your dog will appreciate it.

Part of the care for your retriever is to eat healthily. Studies show that the diet of a

Retriever dog can affect its longevity and overall health. Dogs with a carefully guided diet can live longer than dogs whose food intake is not controlled or modified.

Always consult your veterinarian about the right Golden Retriever diet. You will always be the best person to recommend real beneficial foods for your dog and also human foods to avoid.

Kind reader,

Thank you very much. I hope you enjoyed the book.

Can I ask you a big favor?

I would be grateful if you would please take a few minutes to leave me a gold star on Amazon.

Thank you again for your support.

Kate Liberty

Made in the USA
Las Vegas, NV
04 November 2020